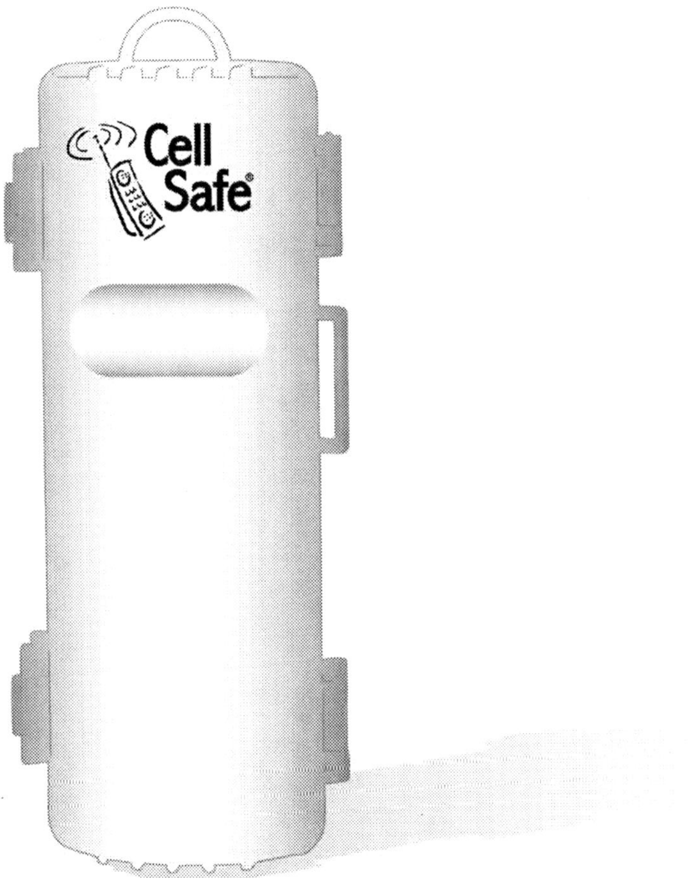
Cell
Safe®

Secrets

of a

Midnight

Entrepreneur

"The true story guide
for turning your idea
into a business."

By James Bowes, Jr.

First published by Dog Ear Publishing
4010 W. 86th Street, Ste H
Indianapolis, IN 46268
www.dogearpublishing.net

ISBN: 1-59858-037-X
Library of Congress Control Number: 2005931077

This book is printed on acid-free paper.

Printed in the United States of America

Introduction

This book is a guide explaining how to turn a product idea into a business using the Philosophy and Tactics of what I call the "Midnight Entrepreneur." It is also the story of how I brought an idea to life and subsequently built a business around it. I have included many of my successes, as well as many of my failures. There are many ways to bring an idea to market; I focus on how to do it yourself. Licensing or selling your idea is a very difficult thing to do; your chances for success are much greater if you take things into your own hands.

At its core, the Philosophy of the Midnight Entrepreneur is fairly simple. Launch your business at night, while still working a full time job. The business world has changed dramatically in recent years. The growth of the Internet and the lower prices of many technologies has made it much easier for a clever and dedicated entrepreneur to launch a business. I was able to use the Internet to aid in the development process, conduct cost-effective marketing, manage the manufacturing and fulfillment process, and build sales. Throughout the book I will share more details on the Tactics and Tools available to the Midnight Entrepreneur.

If you are looking for information on how to get rich quickly, I have bad news. Other than armed robbery or the lottery, there is no way to obtain a lot of money very quickly. However, if you have an idea that you think might make a good product, and you are willing to work hard, this book can help you turn your idea into reality. The process is not quick, and it takes an extensive investment of both time and money. But with hard work and determination, it can be done.

I have had the fortunate experience of working with a variety of startup companies. Some were more successful than others, but each of them offered me a unique learning experience. Somewhere along the line I had a few product ideas and decided to go out on my own and see if I could turn them into my own successful business. I started my first company in 1998. As I write this, it is 2005 and that business is still in operation. It has not made me excessively wealthy, (which, by the way, was the goal). But, it has been profitable (for the most part) and I have enjoyed every minute of the experience!

If you have an idea for a business, and truly believe that you want to see that business become a reality, then the first step is to believe in yourself. Believe in your dream. Other people may try to steer you away, and tell you that you will fail; but you must ignore them. It's up to you to make it happen, no one will do it for you.

The Midnight Philosophy

- *Do not be afraid of hard work. You will learn from experience that hard work is rewarded. Even if you are up until midnight solving a problem, your goal will be met.*

- *As a Midnight Entrepreneur you are not bound by a "standard set of rules" or traditional work hours. You will find the time and resources to make things happen.*
- *Focus on the assets that you have, not the ones that you don't. Don't let a lack of resources prevent you from trying.*
- *Keep your expenses low. You do not need a fancy office or the latest gadgets. Utilize your resources to the full extent, and find bargains on the things you need.*
- *Don't quit the day job until you are really ready.*

Chapter 1

"An Idea Is Born"

Are you an idea person?

So you want to be an inventor, do you? You want to join the ranks of famous inventors, change lives, have an impact on society, and oh yes, become rich at the same time? You are not alone, but the truth is, most inventors give up after a few failures. For some people, they wake up one day, and a light bulb goes off in their head. They have an idea for a product or a service that people "can't live without!" They start daydreaming about their idea, and how the finished product will turn out.

However, unless they can visualize the agony of many defeats, false starts and setbacks, their daydream will turn into a nightmare. As I mentioned earlier, it takes "true grit and determination" to turn an idea from a dream into reality, but it can be done. With an iron will, and a "can't say can't, won't say won't" attitude, you will succeed.

That does not mean you will not run into many obstacles along your journey to success. Remember that Clint Eastwood movie, when he portrayed Dirty Harry? (I'm talking about the original one, not the sequels.) There was a scene early on in the movie, after he had apprehended a suspect who was trying to rob a diner. After the usual shoot out, no one was sure how many shots had been fired. Or how many shots remained in his 357 magnum. His famous line went something like this: "I don't know if I have fired five, or six shots, but the real question you have to ask yourself is this: do you feel lucky?"

Do you feel lucky about your idea?

Of course, we all know how that scene turned out. But that example was from a movie; something that was scripted for entertainment. However, consider these examples of real people who were faced with obstacles, but never gave up:

- In 1954, Elvis Presley was fired from the Grand Ole Opry after only one performance and told by the manager, "You ain't goin' nowhere, son. Better get y'all job back driving a truck."
- Babe Ruth spent his childhood years in an orphanage and then struck out 1,330 times on his way to 714 home runs and baseball immortality.
- In 1933, Walter Cronkite failed an early audition in local radio and was told by the radio station manager that he would never make it as a radio announcer. He went on to become one of America's most recognizable and trusted voices.
- Oprah Winfrey was fired from her reporter's job at a Baltimore television station and was told "you are not fit for TV." Yet she has gone on to become one of the most beloved and successful women in television.

I could go on and on; the world is filled with examples of people who have tried, and failed, but they kept on going. They kept on moving forward, towards their goal. They had a dream and a vision, and they let no setback or failure stop them from seeing their idea turn into reality.

The Midnight Philosophy

- *If you have an idea for a business, you must think that the unachievable can be achieved.*
- *Creative people can come up with an idea. Successful creative people won't get discouraged when obstacles get in the way.*
- *You must be willing to take risks, and believe in yourself. Critical thinking skills are important for every idea.*

The Cell Safe Story: An Idea is Born

I created a product that is marketed under the Registered Trademark of "Cell Safe". It is a shockproof, watertight, floating case for a cellular telephone. It is also designed to mount to the standard water bottle cage that is found on most bicycles. This product was first sold in 1998. The Cell Safe is still in production and hundreds of thousands of them have been sold.

The evolution of the Cell Safe product has a number of interesting steps. In 1995, I quit my job as an engineer at a Helicopter Factory in Connecticut. I moved back to Boston to finish the one class I needed to get a Masters in Manufacturing Engineering from Boston University.

Cell Safe Product Photo

When I resided in Connecticut from 1991 to 1995, I lived very close to the company that makes the Wiffle Ball products. Being a naturally curious person, one day I went over to the factory to check out their operations. I had always been curious about the Wiffle Ball and Bat, and now had a chance to see firsthand how it was made. The factory consisted of one mold machine and two molds, one for the bat and one for the ball. The owner of the factory had this mold running 24/7 for the last 25 years. What a smart man! I decided that one of my objectives in life was to someday create a similar product and business.

Back to 1995. I was 25, single, and living with a few other guys in Boston. At the time, and unlike now, I was very active and often went mountain bike riding. I had a few product ideas at the time, most of them cycling related. When I would go biking, I would always bring two things, some tools and a first aid kit. Something on the bike was always breaking, and somebody was always falling and getting hurt. My bike had two water bottle cages, I would use one for water, but the other was usually empty. I would carry the tools and first aid stuff in a small backpack. One day I got the brilliant idea to shove the tools and first aid stuff into another water bottle, and use the empty cage to carry it. This worked great, but it was a pain to get the stuff in and out of the bottle. I thought, if the bottle opened like a book it would make it much easier. So I came up with a concept for a storage container that opened like a book. I called the product the "Tool-Aid Bottle."

I then started to brainstorm other uses for this type of product. At the time, the cell phone was still fairly large, but the new Motorola Flip Phone fit into the available space. I knew in time phones would get smaller. After some research, I decided that making the case watertight, and hence floating, and focusing solely on the Cell Phone market the product would have wider appeal then a tool case. This product concept matched my original wiffle ball objective (making one mold, and running it forever.)

In 1996, I was working on some other product concepts; mostly ideas that required less startup capital, since I was mostly broke. But, I kept the Cell Safe idea alive and solicited feedback at every opportunity.

Before I continue with the next section of the Cell Safe story, I want to offer some tips on how to turn your idea into something real.

- Many people claim to have come up with an idea for something that they later see in the marketplace. They may have had the idea first, but they did not have what it takes to bring the product to market. ***Find a way!***
- Learn how to brainstorm. Creative people are not afraid of this process. ***Start brainstorming!***
- Start putting your ideas down on paper. Creative people are visual thinkers, so use a large piece of paper or a notebook, and start jotting down those ideas. ***Start writing!***
- Research and create a list of available resources. The Internet makes finding resources a whole lot easier than it was only a decade ago. ***Find those resources!***
- Who is your target audience for your idea? Is it large enough to sustain an investment of your time, energy, and, of course, money? ***Find your target audience!***

Chapter 2

"Get the idea to work"

The Next Step for Cell Safe

The first real steps that I took with the concept involved making a proof of concept mockup of the Cell Safe. I cut up a few plastic water bottles, and started putting different cell phones inside, to see if they would fit. At the time, cell phones were much bigger than they are now, but most of them would fit. This step proved to me that the available space inside a standard water bottle would be big enough to protect and house most cell phones.

The next step involved the creation of a prototype. I took a personal loan from my bank in 1997 for $5,000. With this small investment, I bought a decent computer for just under $2,000, and used the rest to have a tooling shop help me create the prototype. I used some engineering skills to create CAD drawings of the case. (CAD is shorthand for Computer Aided Design.) I then worked with the mold maker to create a rubber mold of the product. If I were to make the prototype today, I would use a newer technology called stereo lithography to "Grow" the part out of a resin. But, at the time it was more cost effective to use the rubber mold technique.

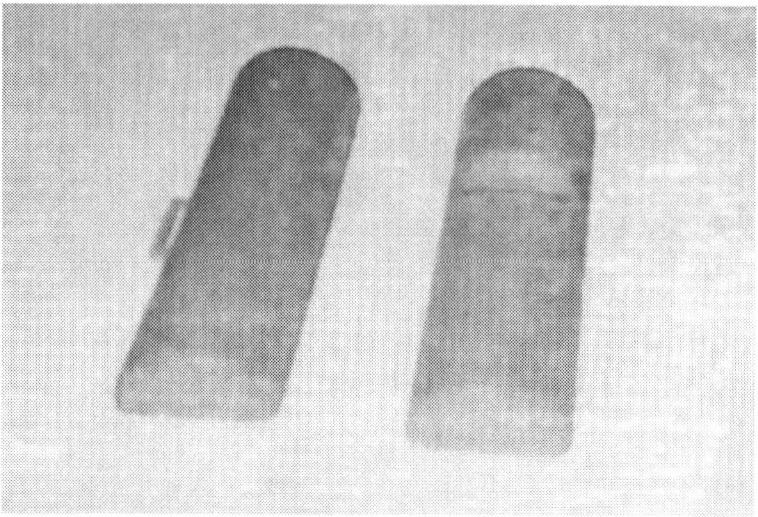

Wood pattern used to make Cell Safe mold.

First Cell Safe Prototype

To make a rubber mold, you first make a wood mock up (pattern) of the product. This pattern is then used to make a rubber negative of that surface. The negative is made by pouring a rubber resin around the pattern. The resin hardens, then you remove the pattern. You can then pour a plastic resin into the hardened mold to create the plastic part. This type of prototyping technique is fairly limited. I was not able to achieve a watertight seal, and the final part is not as durable as an injection molded plastic. But the part looked good and was able to convey the concept of the product. The objective of the prototype was to have a good show and tell piece. Something that we could use to take some marketing photos and use to further sell the concept.

I used the rubber mold to make a total of three prototypes. One was used for nice photographs. The others were used as show and tell and R&D tools. The R&D consisted of me doing field test with the case. This allowed me to develop the optimal interior phone configuration. I also took the case to an acoustics lab to figure out which foam configuration did the least to dampen sound. I wanted the user to be able to hear a phone ringing inside the case. Through some trial and error, I determined the simplest and most effective foam configuration.

At this stage I also created a database of every cell phone on the market. The data included size and weight information. I used this data to figure out what the optimal size of the case should be. The prototype was rather large. The size of the phones was dropping quickly, so I decided that the production version of the case would be smaller than the prototype. The final size had a number of influencing factors, amongst them was the design concept known as the Golden Mean. This concept uses the ratio of 1.61 for the relationship of length and width. This ratio is very popular with artists when they paint. This ratio has a very natural appearance and often has a "Just Looks Right" quality. I tried to come as close as possible to this ratio with the size of the case

The Midnight Philosophy

- *Use the many resources that are available on the Internet to help you locate information and ideas that will help your small business succeed. There are literally millions of pages that have all sorts of business information available for your use. Schedule enough time during your work week to surf the Web and look for information that you can use.*
- *Organization is a key to your success, so it is imperative that you strive to find a way to organize your business so that you can enjoy the fruits of your labor.*
- *Start putting together a team of advisors who are willing to answer your questions and offer suggestions to help your new business succeed.*

Before I continue with the next section of the Cell Safe story, I want to offer some tips on how to become a Midnight Entrepreneur:

Have a strong desire for responsibility – Midnight entrepreneurs feel a personal responsibility for the business they are creating and launching. They are not afraid of responsibility, and are not afraid of delegating tasks when it becomes necessary.

Be open to taking risks – Midnight entrepreneurs are not afraid to take risks. That does not mean they are reckless with resources and people. It just means they are willing to venture outside their comfort zone to make things happen.

Have a high energy level – Midnight entrepreneurs have more energy than the average person. They have the incredible ability to work long hours and never seem to get tired. However, the really smart midnight entrepreneurs have also learned how to take care of themselves by eating right, getting enough sleep and exercising on a daily basis.

Be flexible – Midnight Entrepreneurs are willing to learn and adjust along the way. They understand that it is okay to make changes, as long as they help achieve the end goal.

Have the right attitude – Midnight Entrepreneurs are known to be upbeat and positive. In other words, they have the right attitude.

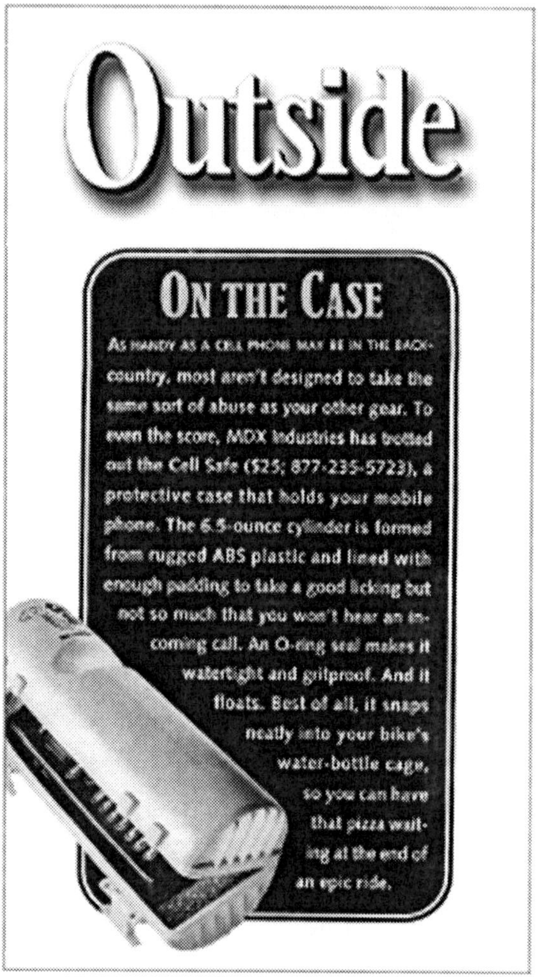

Outside

ON THE CASE

AS HANDY AS A CELL PHONE MAY BE IN THE BACK-country, most aren't designed to take the same sort of abuse as your other gear. To even the score, MDX Industries has bottled out the Cell Safe ($25; 877-235-5723), a protective case that holds your mobile phone. The 6.5-ounce cylinder is formed from rugged ABS plastic and lined with enough padding to take a good licking but not so much that you won't hear an incoming call. An O-ring seal makes it watertight and gritproof. And it floats. Best of all, it snaps neatly into your bike's water-bottle cage, so you can have that pizza waiting at the end of an epic ride.

Cell Safe Appearance in Outside Magazine

Chapter 3

"Patents *Are* Important!"

Why a Midnight Entrepreneur Needs to Have a Patent

Dozens of books have been written about patents, and why they are important. (I know, because I read many of them while researching the patent process!) If you have an idea for a new business, and truly want to be a Midnight Entrepreneur, then you need to understand what a patent is, and how it can protect you and your new business. Here are a few Questions and Answers about patents. (Pay close attention; there may be a quiz at the end of this chapter!!)

Question: What is a patent? Answer: A patent is a property right granted by the Government of the United States of America to an inventor "to exclude others from making, using, offering for sale, or selling the invention throughout the United States or importing the invention into the United States" for a limited time in exchange for public disclosure of the invention when the patent is granted. (This is a *very important point; read it again!*)

Question: Who can apply for a patent?Answer: A patent may be applied for in the name of the inventor (or inventors).

Question: What can and cannot be patented?Answer: What ***can*** be patented – utility patents are provided for a new, non-obvious and useful:

- Process
- Machine
- Article of manufacture
- Composition of matter
- Improvement of any of the above

What **cannot** be patented:

- Laws of nature
- Physical phenomena
- Abstract ideas
- Literary, dramatic, musical, and artistic works (these can be Copyright protected).
- Inventions which are not useful, or offensive to public morality.

Cell Safe Patent Story..

For me the patent process started with another product. Being a true Midnight Entrepreneur, prior to launching Cell Safe I had a number of ideas that I tried to develop. One of these was a brake light for a bicycle. Similar to a car, the lights would come on when the brakes were applied to a bike. I came up with a concept, and tinkered with it until I had a working product. My objective for this project was simple, take an idea from my head all the way to market, do all of the steps in between, and not lose too much money. I wound up reading a few books on the patent process and doing quite a bit of patent research. I completed a patent application for this product, but never filed it. Along the way, I realized the marketability of this product would not support the production costs, but I achieved my goal of learning about the process. (I could write another entire book on the "Midnight Brake Light The Bicycle Brake Light Project!)

As for Cell Safe, I did some preliminary research, and was eventually introduced to a high profile patent lawyer through a mutual friend. He agreed to help in the process, but, I was not able to afford his full time attention. He gave me a book to read. *Patent It Yourself* by David Pressman. This book gave excellent instruction on the patent process. I had already filed for a provisional patent on my own. This gave me one year to get the formal application completed. Using the book, I wrote out the entire application myself. I then had the patent lawyer review it and provide direction and guidance. So I wrote most of it myself, but had some experienced supervision.

Key Phases of the Patent Process

1. Patent Search: You can do a preliminary search at the Patent Office Website. www.uspto.gov. Using the search tools at this site, do a keyword search on any descriptions that you can think of for your idea. I guarantee something relevant will turn up. Read as many patents as you can. You will notice that many patents reference other prior patents, they will also mention other patents that use it as a reference. It is a good idea to look at all of these.

2. Provisional Patent Application: This item was designed to allow the individual inventor a method to protect an idea, without having to go through the expense of the full application. It is a simple disclosure of the idea. By filing this application, you establish a filing date. You then have one year to complete the full application. This period is designed to allow the inventor time to further research the idea, including presenting it to other companies for development. If the idea does not prove fruitful, you can abandon the initial application and not incur further costs.

3. Final Patent Application: This step is the most detailed and time consuming. If you decided that your idea is firstly, Patentable, and secondly, serves a viable commercial need, then it is worth your time to push forward with the application. The key to this step is to do

a thorough job explaining why your product is unique and different from prior inventions. It is a good idea to envision future versions of your idea and try to patent as many as possible.

I have received three separate Patents. I have had many other ideas, but only these three had enough marketability for me to pursue. Each one has spawned a profitable product that has made it into a major retail outlet.

My first patent was for the "Cell Safe" Phone case. This patent took the longest time to get. Due to turnover at the patent office, I had to deal with 4 different examiners over the course of three years. After an initial rejection, eventually the patent was issued.

During the process for my second and third patents I did not use a patent attorney for guidance, I did it entirely myself. Each of these applications was initially rejected, but through persistence and some modifications eventually the patents were issued. These patents were for my "ClipSafe" and "KeyCover" products.

The Midnight Philosophy

- *Leverage your resources. Find qualified people to help you. If you can afford to hire a patent attorney, it is worth it to do so. If you can't afford to hire experts, look around, you probably have friends that can help. I had a friend who was a technical artist. He helped me with some of the drawings for the patent application.*

US006092707A

United States Patent [19]

Bowes, Jr.

[11] **Patent Number:** **6,092,707**

[45] **Date of Patent:** **Jul. 25, 2000**

[54] **SHOCK AND WEATHER PROTECTIVE MOBILE TELEPHONE CASE**

[76] Inventor: **James Bowes, Jr.**, P.O. Box 1268, Marblehead, Mass. 01945

[21] Appl. No.: **08/936,697**

[22] Filed: **Sep. 24, 1997**

Related U.S. Application Data

[60] Provisional application No. 60/037,936, Feb. 14, 1997.

[51] **Int. Cl.**[7] **B62J 11/00**

[52] **U.S. Cl.** **224/435**; 224/431; 224/929; 206/320; 206/523

[58] **Field of Search** 224/428, 430, 224/431, 433, 435, 414, 412, 440, 441, 451--456, 457, 459--462, 148.3, 929; 206/523, 305, 320, 372

[56] **References Cited**

U.S. PATENT DOCUMENTS

3,263,806	8/1966	Ring	224/148.3
3,578,199	5/1971	Duncan	224/148.3
3,777,882	12/1973	McIntyre	206/372
3,904,058	9/1975	Rosenstein	206/523
4,193,525	3/1980	Sommers	224/435
4,836,374	6/1989	Hutchins et al.	206/523
4,865,186	9/1989	Gates .	
5,016,749	5/1991	Raye .	
5,114,060	5/1992	Boyer	224/435
5,159,712	10/1992	Schneider et al.	224/929
5,178,308	1/1993	Endre .	
5,251,777	10/1993	McMahon	224/433
5,320,223	6/1994	Allen	206/523
5,388,691	2/1995	White .	
5,417,327	5/1995	Saumure	224/148.3

OTHER PUBLICATIONS

Allied Bicycle Tool Set in water bottle case; model 69090, 1996.

Primary Examiner—Gregory M. Vidovich

[57] **ABSTRACT**

A shock and weather protective telephone case, composed of two separate halves which when mated together form a hollow cylinder with capped ends. A mobile telephone or other similarly sized equipment is protected by placing it within the cylinder. The body of the case includes an indentation to secure the case to a standard bicycle water bottle holder. The case provides a waterproof seal with which to protect the contents. Foam inserts are located on the internal walls of the cylinder to secure and protect the contents from shock and also allow acoustical clearance.

6 Claims, 15 Drawing Sheets

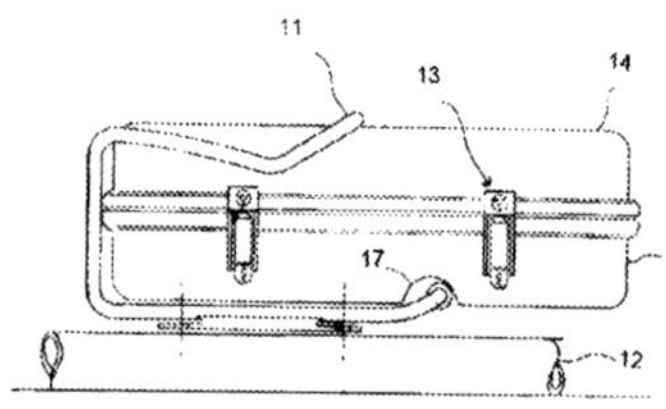

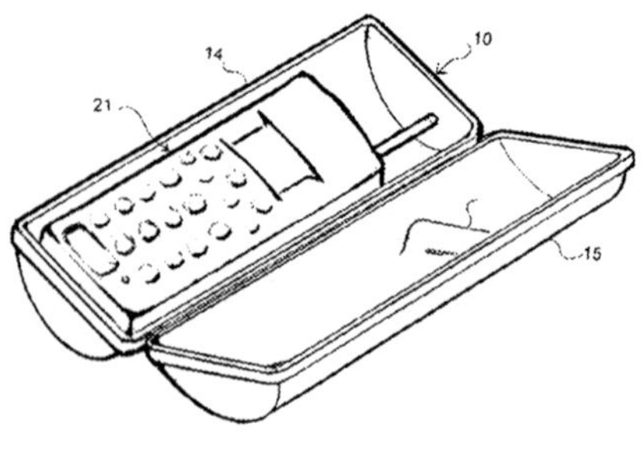

- *Don't be easily discouraged. If you find out that your idea has already been patented, check the date on the patent, it may be expired. Also check the status, the patent owner may have forfeited the patent by not paying the maintenance fees. Just because someone else has already had your idea it doesn't mean that you can't proceed. You just may have to do it without a Patent of your own.*
- *Avoid "Invention Companies" that promise to help bring your idea to market for a fee. There are a bunch of them out there. My experience is that they will do nothing for you. Their success rate for bringing products to market is ridiculously small. They are in the business of getting you to pay them fees.*

Trademarks

Registering and protecting your product name is almost as important as patenting the technology of your product. You will need to create an identity for both your product and your company. Depending on the type of product that you create, the name will be very important. You will invest a lot of time and energy to build awareness for your product, it is wise to find ways to prevent other companies from copying your name.

Similar to the Patent process, the trademark process will begin with a search of currently Registered Trademarks at the www.uspto.gov website. If you don't find any conflicting trademarks, you can then complete the application process completely online.

Trademark protection itself is quite different than Patent protection. When you register your trademark you will have to select a category for your product. Based on the type of name you choose, there may be other identical names trademarked for other industries. I registered the Trademark “Cell Safe” for use with protective cases for electronics. There is another “Cell Safe” registered by another company for use as a container for holding biological samples.

The Patent and Trademark Office will grant a Trademark registration on the same term to different companies if it thinks that the markets served are distinct enough to prevent any confusion in the marketplace.

Chapter 4

Who Wants It? – Market Research

What is Market Research, and why is it important?

Market research is a systematic, objective collection and analysis of data about your target market, competition, and/or environment. Through the market research process, you can take *data*–a variety of related or non-related facts–and create useful *information* to guide your business decisions. Market research is not an activity conducted only once; it is an ongoing study.

Benefits of Market Research

Information gained through marketing research isn't just "nice to know." It's solid information that can guide your most important strategic business decisions. Market research is effective when the findings or conclusions you reach have a value that exceeds the cost of the research itself. For example, if you spend $500 on market research activities that yields information leading to a revenue increase of $5,000, the research was well worth it! Suppose you spend $500 on a customer survey that uncovers an unmet customer need. You'll have the opportunity to offer a new product or service (or alter your existing product or service) to meet the need and gain new revenues.

Cell Safe Story: How I Became a Market Research Expert

My market research had a few phases. The first phase was mostly word of mouth questioning. Originally I started pitching the idea to bicycle shop owners, and they loved the idea. I then started polling a few cell phone stores. Most people were receptive to the idea of the product. This phase was fairly informal and not very scientific. At the same time, I was still researching the feasibility of the product, determining which phones would fit and which ones would not. I also quantified the size of the market. I was able to obtain data on cell phone usage and its growth rate. I also found data on how many people participated in different outdoor activities. From this information, I was able to quantify the number of potential customers. Some of this market data was included in the initial business plan.

The second phase of the market research came after I had the prototypes. I had some nice pictures taken, and then sent out a limited press release. The objective was to see what type or response the industry and consumers would give to the product. We got placements in a few magazines, and we then got many calls from dealers that were interested in carrying the product. The response was overwhelmingly positive. I very carefully logged these calls and had some very informative discussions with all of the dealers that wanted to carry the product. I informed each customer that the product was currently on back order, (a small variation of the truth), and that

I would contact them as soon as the product became available.

Normally you should send out a press release once you have product available to sell. It is not wise to create a demand that you cannot fill. But, as a Midnight Entrepreneur, I had very little to lose from this market probing tactic. The data gained from the premature press release proved to me that there was a market for the product. It was well worth further investments of my time and funds.

Picture of Cell Safe prototype that was sent out with press release

Midnight Advice

My advice to others is to be careful when doing the research. It is important to understand how many potential consumers there are, but it is equally important to understand the distribution methods needed to reach these consumers. I focused on consumers and retail dealers. In hindsight, I would have also spent more time talking to independent sales reps, and to major distributors. I contacted these guys much later in the process.

Understanding the distribution channels for your market is critical to your success. There are many different methods of distribution, and each has its own specific pricing expectations. You need to research and understand your market.

What Market Research Can Tell You

- *Market segmentation studies* provide information about the characteristics shared by your customers. This data provides answers to questions such as: Who are my customers? What is the size of their population? What percentage is female? What are their ages, races, income and education levels? What are their occupations, skills, interests and hobbies? How many children do they have? Do they have pets? Where do they live and work?

- *Purchasing power and buying habits* information uncovers the financial strengths and economic attributes shared by your target market. Some questions to be answered include: What is the average dollar amount spent on purchases or products or services similar to mine? What are the financing needs of my target market? What is their current usage of my services? When do they purchase? Where do they shop? Why do they decide to buy? How often do they buy? How much do they buy at a time? Do they own or rent their homes? What types of cars do they drive? How often do they eat out? How do they typically spend their disposable income? What methods of payment do they use? How strong is their credit?

- *Psychological aspects of the market* is information regarding the perceived opinions and values held and shared by consumers in your market. Questions to be answered: What is the reaction of the market to my programs or services? How does the market compare my company to other businesses? What qualities and characteristics do my customers deem important? Who makes the decisions to buy in the family or company? What are the deciding factors in making a purchase? Do they only want the best for their family? Are they looking for convenience and time-saving devices? Are they concerned with how they're perceived by others? What are their unmet needs? Do they demand intensive customer service? Are they only concerned with the lowest price? What media (magazines, radio, TV, newspapers, Internet providers, etc.) are they exposed to? What confuses my customers and prospects?

- *Marketplace competition* is information about the other companies within your area of business. Research answers these questions: Who are my primary competitors in the market? How do they compete with me? In what ways do they not compete with me? What are their strengths and weaknesses? Are there profitable opportunities based upon their weaknesses? What is their market niche? What makes my business unique from the others? How do my competitors position themselves? How do they communicate their services to the market? Who are their customers? How are they perceived by the market? Who are the industry leaders? What is their sales volume? Where are they located? Are they profitable?

- *Environmental factors* information uncovers, economical and political circumstances that can influence your productivity and operations. Questions to be answered include: What are the current and future population trends? What are the current and future socio-economic trends? What effects do economic and political policies have on the target market or my industry? What are the growth expectations for my market? What outside factors influence the industry's performance?

What are the trends for this market and for the economy? Is the industry growing, at a plateau, or declining?

Men's Health

TRAVEL GEAR

A Watertight Case

The Cell Safe is a crushproof, waterproof plastic container for your cell phone that fits into your bike's water-bottle holder. It's lined with shock-absorbing foam that won't dull the phone's ringing, and it has room for money, ID, and keys, too. $25. To order, call (877) 235-5723.

www.menshealth.com

JUNE 1999 **49** MEN'S HEALTH

Appearance in Men's Health Magazine

Chapter 5

Ready to Make It!

You have a great idea, but how do you make it work?

By now, many of you who are reading this book have already started taking notes, and hopefully, as I continue to tell the Cell Safe story, you will be inspired to launch your own product soon. However, I know that many of you are also scratching your head, trying to figure out another important step in the process. *I have this great idea for a product, but just how the heck do I have a prototype or a model made?*

Good question, and I have a good answer: ***research!*** The Internet is always a good place to begin. Your local telephone book yellow pages are another source that can provide information on potential manufacturers. Before you contact anyone, make sure you have a rock solid idea of what it is you want them to create. If you cannot put your design down on paper quite yet, then you are not ready for this phase of the process, but keep trying, and don't give up.

Cell Safe Story Continues...

My own mold company story is very interesting. My occupation at the time, Manufacturing Manager at an electronic startup company, put in me in contact with many manufacturing companies. There was a company that I was dealing with that I liked and knew could do a good job. But, due to the fact that I was moonlighting this project, I did not approach them about the product; I did not want any conflict of interest type situations to develop. At the time I was secretly pursuing the Cell Safe product, the management at my day job did not know about it. So, I contacted a number of other molding companies. At the time I looked them up in the Thomas Register, which is now available online, but then it was in a bunch of books. This register is a directory of all the manufacturing companies in the United States. It is sorted geographically, and by category. So I found a few other similar companies in the area, and started asking for quotes. At the time, I would give them my CAD drawings of the product, plus show them the prototypes. I received a number of quotes, most of them a bit out of my reach. The big challenge was the cost of making the mold. Most of the quotes were in the $40k range.

I needed the mold company to do a few things. One, refine my design so that it worked as an injection molded part. Two, fabricate the mold. And three, mold the production parts. There were a total of four individual plastic parts. The front and back of the case, and the two latches. The mold would be designed so that all four parts would be molded with one shot of plastic.

At some point in the quoting process I was approached by the salesman at the molding company I was using for my day job. He told me how he and the two other key guys from our project at his company were quitting to go start their own company. They were hoping that I would bring the business to their new company. They did not yet know that the product they were working on for us was being shipped overseas, and that their piece of the business was going away. But, at this time, I decided that their new company quoting the Cell Safe product would not be a conflict of interest.

I approached them, and they provided a much better quote on the project. They did not have much other business yet, and were willing to do the mold design and fabrication work at a low price in order to get the production work that would come afterwards. They did a great job, and were very helpful. However, a few years later, I had to transfer production of the product overseas to China, due to pricing and competitive issues.

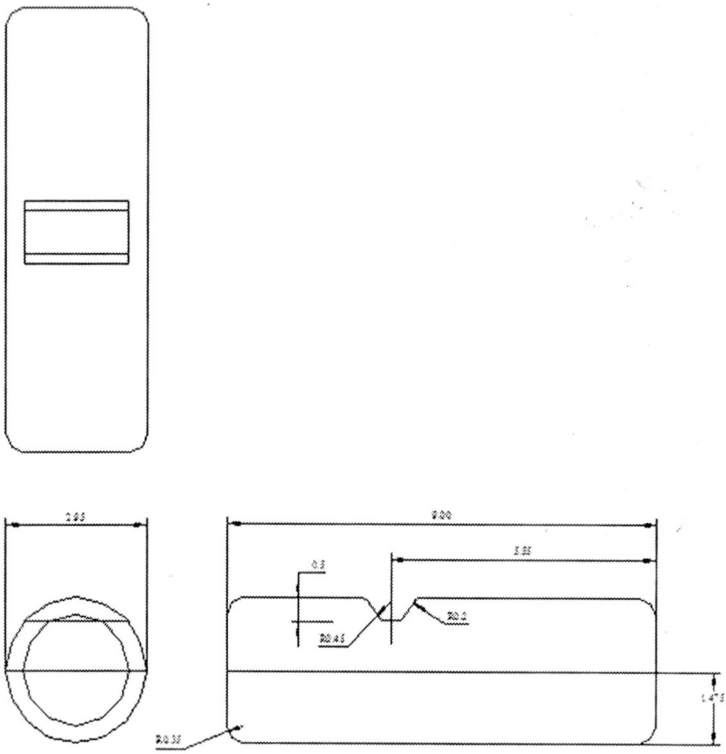

Early CAD design of the Cell Safe

Midnight Advice

- *Once you have a prototype, go visit the potential manufacturers. You will learn a lot about manufacturing, so start visiting different factories.*
- *Be professional. Dress appropriately and look the part. Have business cards. The salesman at these facilities will give you better service if you appear to have your act together. If they think you are wasting their time, they won't be very helpful.*
- *Be truthful. Never lie and sugarcoat your situation. It will only hurt you in the long run. Let them know that you are an entrepreneur and that this is a new venture.*
- *Have a presentation, or some marketing materials to help explain the product. Also, be ready to talk about the market demand for the product. The manufacturers will immediately want to know what quantities to quote. Also, if you can, explain your financing. If they know that you have money, they will respond immediately. If they believe in your business plan, they may even be willing to invest or provide service in exchange for equity. This can be a good thing, but you should never bring this up in the first meeting. Let them t[illegible] that you don't need them. This will give you a [illegible] position.*

- *Get multiple quotes. Never jump on the first quote. You may go back to them eventually, but it is a good practice to get at least three quotes.*
- *Ask about other services. A mold shop that can also do assembly and packaging may be a very cost-effective way to make your product. I only had the mold company make the plastic. I then had another company print the logo on the product. The printing company eventually did the assembly and packaging of the product. The objective is having the most cost effective supply chain. Moving parts from building to building takes time and money.*
- *Understand payment terms: Some companies want deposits. Some demand payment at delivery. Others will give Net 30 terms. You always want terms. They may ask you to fill out a credit application to get terms. You will need trade references, this will be hard when you first start out, but is important.*
- *Understand shipping costs: Freight costs as part of the manufacturing process, need to be considered when determining the true cost of the product.*
- *Don't order too many pieces. In the early days the product may still be evolving, never commit to more inventory than you have to. Sometimes it's better to ship product a little late, then to have thousands of items that you can't sell.*

If I had to do it over again, what would I do differently?

When I started this process, I had different companies quote the different pieces. I had a total of seven vendors for the following components:

1. Hinge Pins
2. Foam Insert and O-ring
3. Printing and Assembly
4. Insert Card
5. Plastic Parts
6. Boxes and packaging
7. Velcro Straps

For the first few years, I would order all the parts, have them shipped to the printer, who would assemble and package them. I now have the product turn-key assembled over in China. "Turn-Key" is a term used if the contract manufacturer provides a completed, ready to ship product.

If I had to do this all over again, I would find a company to turn-key assemble from the beginning. I spent too much time managing the different pieces of the supply chain. There are many local companies that could have done the complete job in the beginning. This would have freed up time for me to do other things. I blame this strategy on the engineer in me. was well experienced with this type of production coordir tion, but in hindsight there was no value to me doing

Even if the product cost were slightly more, I would have profited from having the time to focus on marketing and sales.

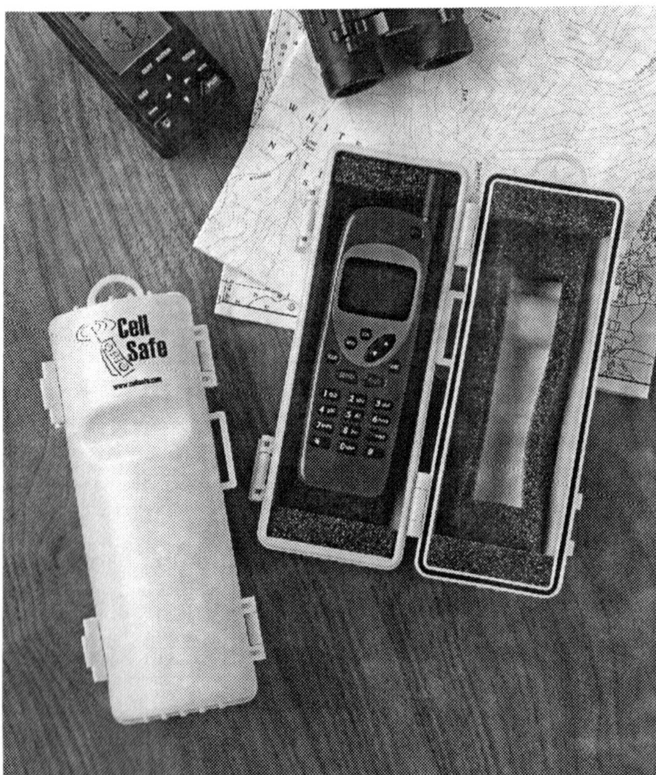

First marketing photographs of the production Cell Safe.

Chapter 6:

Slow Down, It is Time for a Business Plan!

Business Plan Basics

A business plan precisely defines your business, identifies your goals, and serves as your firm's resume. The basic components include a current and pro forma balance sheet, an income statement, and a cash flow analysis. It helps you allocate resources properly, handle unforeseen complications, and make good business decisions. Because it provides specific and organized information about your company and how you will repay borrowed money, a good business plan is a crucial part of any loan application. Additionally, it informs sales personnel, suppliers, and others about your operations and goals.

The importance of a comprehensive, thoughtful business plan cannot be overemphasized. Much hinges on it: outside funding, credit from suppliers, management of your operation and finances, promotion and marketing of your business, and achievement of your goals and objectives.

Despite the critical importance of a business plan, many entrepreneurs drag their feet when it comes to preparing a written document. They argue that their marketplace changes too fast for a business plan to be useful or that they just don't have enough time. But just as a builder won't begin construction without a blueprint, eager business owners shouldn't rush into new ventures without a business plan.

Before you begin writing your business plan, consider four core questions:

- What service or product does your business provide and what needs does it fill?
- Who are the potential customers for your product or service and why will they purchase it from you?
- How will you reach your potential customers?
- Where will you get the financial resources to start your business?

Writing the Plan

What goes in a business plan? The body can be divided into four distinct sections:

1) Description of the business

2) Marketing

3) Finances

4) Management

Addenda should include an executive summary, supporting documents, and financial projections. Although there is no single formula for developing a business plan, some elements are common to all business plans. They are summarized in the following outline:

Elements of a Business Plan

1. **Cover sheet**
2. **Executive summary**
3. **Table of contents**

I. The Business

A. Description of business

B. Marketing

C. Competition

D. Operating procedures

E. Personnel

F. Business insurance

II. Financial Data

A. Loan applications

B. Capital equipment and supply list

C. Balance sheet

D. Breakeven analysis

E. Pro-forma income projections (profit & loss statements)

a. Three-year summary

b. Detail by month, first year

c. Detail by quarters, second and third years

F. Pro-forma cash flow

III. Supporting Documents

- Tax returns of principals for last three years
- Personal financial statement (all banks have these forms)
- Copy of proposed lease or purchase agreement for building space
- Copy of licenses and other legal documents
- Copy of resumes of all principals
- Copies of letters of intent from suppliers, etc.

The Cell Safe story....

We catch up with the Cell Safe story at a very crucial juncture. I have a few prototypes, I have applied for a patent, I have researched the market, and I have now received some good quotes on actually manufacturing the product. What I am lacking is the money to launch the business. I know from my experience with other start-up companies that I will need to find someone to invest in this new venture.

The first step to finding investors is to have a thorough and concise business plan. I put together a package with a plan, pictures of the prototype, and a toy phone with the Cell Safe logo on it. I put the items in a nice box and sent them out to 25 potential investors. Within 6 weeks I had achieved my target goal, and wound up turning down some potential investors.

These investors were mostly friends and business associates. This type of investment round is sometimes called a 3F fundraiser. The F's are Family, Friends and Fools. The investors all had faith in my abilities, which is the key to raising money. Your plan must be sound, but in the end, investors are really investing in the management team of the company. I was able to put together a board of advisors and recruited a strong marketing and sales consultant. This experienced team provided quite a bit of credibility to my business plan.

I was able to raise the funding I needed to launch the business. But a key part of the plan indicated that rather soon after launching I would need to raise additional capital. I had already researched obtaining a Small Business Administration loan (SBA). A simple explanation of an SBA loan is that the SBA, if they approve your plan and you meet certain criteria, will serve as a cosigner on the loan. The SBA will back plans for growing a business, but will not invest in a pure startup. They want to see sales data and other performance measures.

A second version of the business plan was created a year after the business was launched. This version was mostly an update of the original plan, but rather than projected sales and revenue data, we were able to show actual information. By this time we needed more working capital to help finance inventory. We applied for and received an SBA backed loan, through a local community bank. I had spoken with many larger banks, but they were difficult to approach and did not seem very interested in working with a small business. The Ipswich Co-op Bank, (Ipswich, MA) was extremely helpful during the application process and has become a key partner in the success of the business.

Sample Executive Summary

On the opposite page is one iteration of the Executive Summary of the Cell Safe business plan. This version was used with our application for the SBA business loan. Note that this one page document explains who we are, what we want, our accomplishments to date, and the exact use of the funds that we are requesting. The rest of the business plan provides more detail to the areas summarized on this sheet.

This document makes reference to a company called "MDX". This is the name of our company. Cell Safe is the name of the product.

I
Executive Summary

Business

MDX is in the business of outdoor safety and communications. The first product in the line is Cell Safe, potentially explosive, representing a perfect marriage of two booming consumer interests; those 186,000,000 Americans pursuing outdoor activities, combined with the their compulsive urge to stay in reach of communication. 61,000,000 Americans are using mobile cellular telephones. The market is growing and there is no competition.

Product

With the patent pending, Cell Safe consumers can take their phones anywhere, safely. Cellular telephones are sensitive electronics, adverse to water and are not durable for outdoor activities. Impact resistant Cell Safe is designed specifically to solve this problem. Made in the USA out of rugged, bright yellow, ABS plastic, Cell Safe is watertight and shock resistant. Fitting conveniently in any lightweight "water bottle cage," Cell Safe provides a $25 dollar solution to a common problem. Phone and outdoor enthusiasts love it!

Forecast

MDX's persistent and creative inventor, Engineer, James Bowes Jr., has Cell Safe in full production. We are ready to meet an explosive demand. MDX is projecting sales of 72,000 units for 1999 and to sell over 250,000 Cell Safe units in 2000.

Marketing

MDX has enlisted the services of OPT4 to manage the marketing and sales strategy, lead by seasoned marketing expert, Scott Taylor. Since receiving his MBA from Harvard in 1981 Scott has successfully rolled out numerous products and been involved directly in the growth of two successful small businesses. Marketing efforts have generated a great "buzz" about Cell Safe. It has been featured in Outside Magazine, Men's Health Magazine, Boating Magazine and is slated for Field & Stream, Men's Journal, Wired Magazine and several other main stream publications. Every exposure has lead to 100's of units being sold. OPT4 is building a strong mail-order presence in national catalogs like Herringtons, Overtons, Cabela's and others. Circulation of these catalogs typically reach 9-10 million consumers annually.

Sales

Strong interest has been expressed by leading national retail chains including REI, EMS and Brookstone. OPT4 is adding secondary retailers and sporting goods shops daily and expects to amass several hundred outlets by the 1999 Christmas buying season. Success has been the result of a persistent telephone and sampling campaign and a presence at relevant trade shows.

Structure

MDX is a classic 90's company. No money is wasted on facilities. We have a strong Web presence and our management team communicates via e-mail and monthly meetings. Our manufacturing is all subcontracted, and our distribution strategy brings the product directly into our customer's home.

Finance

Investors shouldered the risky aspect of our business, including the product development and launch. Now we need to finance our growth. Cell Safe is creating a huge demand and filling the product void is critical. To effectively manage the working capital cycle and year-end Christmas buying surge, we are seeking to establish a strong banking relationship including a loan of $100,000.

Chapter 7

"Don't Forget Sales and Marketing"

Understanding Marketing

In plain and simple terms, marketing activities and strategies result in making products available that satisfy customers while making profits for the companies that offer those products. That's it in a nutshell! Marketing produces a "win-win" because:

- Customers have a product that meets their needs, and
- Healthy profits are achieved for the company. (These profits allow the company to continue to do business in order to meet the needs of future customers.)

Stated another way: A focus on what the customer wants is essential to successful marketing efforts. This customer-orientation must also be balanced with the company's objective of maintaining a profitable volume of sales in order for the company to continue to do business. Marketing is a creative, ever-changing orchestration of all the activities needed to accomplish both of these objectives.

How Are The Customer And Business Objectives Met?

The American Marketing Association's definition of marketing is:

the process of planning and executing the conception, pricing, promotion and distribution of ideas, goods, and services to create exchanges that satisfy individual and organizational objectives.

You see in the above definition that the process of marketing begins with discovering what product customers want to buy. Providing the features and quality customers want is a *critical* first step in marketing. You'll be facing an uphill battle if you provide something *you want to produce* and then try to *convince* someone to buy it. The marketing process then continues with setting a price, letting potential customers know about your product, and making it available to them.

What activities are included in marketing?

Marketing activities are numerous and varied because they basically include everything needed to get a product off the drawing board and into the hands of the customer. The broad field of marketing includes activities such as designing the product so it will be desirable to customers (using tools such as marketing research and pricing; promoting the product so people will know about it (using tools such as public relations, advertising, marketing communications; and exchanging it with the customer (through sales and distribution.) It is important to note that the field of marketing *includes* sales, but it also includes many functions besides sales. Many people mistakenly think that marketing and sales are the same, they are not. Another way to describe marketing activities is to consider the big picture of how they fit in with the other business functions.

- Through **marketing** efforts, decisions are made and strategies are implemented concerning:
    1. what products (goods, services or ideas) are to be offered
    2. to whom (the target market)
    3. how (how to inform potential customers of the offering, how to make the transaction, etc.)
- Products are created through **production** efforts.
- Capital and operating funds are managed and tracked in the **accounting/finance** area.
- The focus of the **human resources** area is employees and the policies concerning them.

Oftentimes, a marketing approach relies upon the coordination of several business areas to be successful. For example,

- The product might need some tweaking by the person who produces the product to respond to customer complaints.
- The person who handles human resource issues might be asked to develop compensation plans that reward sales people who build significant relationships that have tremendous potential but are slow to close.

- Special payment plans might need to be implemented by the accounting staff to accommodate a variety of customer needs.

As a result, marketing usually crosses more departmental boundaries than other business functions. So, marketing requires the orchestration of everyone who plays a part in the common goal of pleasing the customer. For a small business owner who has no employees, this means that she needs to mentally tear down the walls between varied business functions and think holistically when it comes to marketing strategies.

The Midnight Philosophy

These are the fundamentals of a true marketing mindset:

- *Producing what the customer wants should be the focus of business operations and planning.*
- *Creating profitable sales volume, not just sales volume, is a necessary goal.*
- *Coordinating between marketing activities and all other functions within a business is a priority.*

The Cell Safe Story Continues…

My first code name for the product was "Cell Shock". My thought was to let people know that the product was meant to protect the phone from shock. At this point I had not yet added the watertight seal. After we added the seal, we saw that the value of the product was not just in the shock protection, but also protecting from water and other elements. We did the normal brainstorming exercise, where we listed as many names as possible. The simplest, and most direct to the point was Cell Safe. "Cell" let them know that it was for a phone, and "Safe" indicated protection.

We had two thoughts on the naming process. One was to give a nondescript name, that might make a good brand, like "Croakies" for the sunglass straps. The second was to give a more to the point name, which explained the product. We settled on the straight to the point name. We wanted the name to explain the product. Just looking at the case, someone might not get that it was a phone case. We thought the name might clarify the purpose of the product.

Identifying the use of the product quickly is important in a retail setting, where your customer might only glimpse the product for a second or two on the shelf. Our first all yellow Cell Safe did very well as a catalog item, but struggled at retail. We eventually added a clear version of the product, which allowed us to put an insert card showing a phone, this version had a much stronger presence at retail and sales were noticeably better.

Public Relations (PR)

Cell Safe did very well in the PR world, with hundreds of free media placements. Part of the reason for this success was the large target market of the product. Cell phones are everywhere, and unique cell phone accessories are fairly rare. We had a lot of good marketing photographs to offer the magazines. We also learned that many magazines are desperate for new gadgets to review. The Cell Safe is a unique enough item, having a strong marketing statement "Keep your phone safe, so that it will work in an emergency, when you really need it", and every magazine knew that most of its subscribers had cell phones. PR came easy for this product.

We targeted publications in the marine, outdoor, general interest, bicycling, camping, fishing, and hunting industries.

Midnight Advice on PR

- *Have a compelling message. We had the safety pitch.*
- *Have a good one page press release.*
- *Send or offer samples. The gadget reviewers expect samples. Be prepared to send them.*
- *Have good digital photos and have product descriptions written. Make it easy for media to include your product in their publication.*

Sales

Early on I knew that sales as a skill set, was my weak link. I had some experience, but not enough in my mind to be successful. Very early in the process, I pitched the concept to Scott Taylor. I had met Scott at Sensitech, my employer at the time. He was a graduate of the Harvard Business School, and a highly regarded sales and marketing expert. He left Sensitech before I launched Cell Safe. He and a partner had their own sales management consulting company. They were involved in a number of projects and had some significant success stories. He liked the Cell Safe project and agreed to get involved. Together we put together the first marketing plan. This happened long before we had the real product; at this time I had one prototype.

The core of the first marketing plan was to pitch the product to the phone companies as a promotional piece. They put their logo on it, and give it away to new subscribers. Our rational was that besides being a desirable freebie for the consumer, it was also smart for the phone company to help people protect their phones. At the time, most phone plans were minute based. If someone lost or damaged their phone, then they would have down time where they would not be making calls, and the phone company would lose revenue. Also, by making it easier to take the phone more places, it would generate more calls, and hence more revenues. Our hope was that they would place a large order, and that we could use this order as leverage to borrow the funds to create the production tooling.

We pitched this plan to all of the large phone companies. They all loved the product, but none would go in for the promo. For a variety of reasons, but mostly because of how the independent dealers were incentivized, no large company would commit. Thus the first sale and marketing effort of Cell Safe proved to be a bust.

Luckily for the product, this was our first, but not our only effort. In parallel to the promotional pitch effort, we also did a targeted press release to the marine industry. This led to quite a few calls from dealers who wanted to carry the product, and we carefully measured this market interest. The strong response from the marine dealers, encouraged us enough to push forward with the product. We pushed forward and formalized the business plan and raised the money to launch the product.

Once we had a target date for production, we started to heavily market the product. The sales consulting company handled most of the phone work, while I handled the logistics. In addition to the marine segment, we also targeted the mail order catalog industry. Mail order companies are famous for being early adopters of new products.

We expected the mold to be ready in early October 1998. We committed to attending the Boating Industry, tradeshow in October. We also had one mail order catalog put the product in their 1998 Fall catalog. They published a picture of the prototype, and had faith that we would have the product ready in time.

My business plan, and fundraising had enough money planned to attend the Boating show and to assemble 2,000 pieces of product. I had planned to sell half of the product, and use the rest as sales samples and promos. The first catalog placement wound up buying all 2,000 pieces of that first run. This greatly aided my early cash flow, financed the production of the next few thousand pieces, and paid for the next trade show. That first trade show gained us two important customers, Overtons, the largest boating catalog, and West Marine, the largest boating retail chain.

The next tradeshow we went to was the Sporting Goods Supershow held in Atlanta. This was in February of 1999. This show helped to land us a few major mail order catalogs, and get into REI, a large outdoor sporting goods chain. Also, this month, we had a major PR appearance in Outside Magazine. This appearance gave us tremendous credibility and exposure. By the end of this month it was clear that I would have to quit the day job.

In 1999 and 2000 we hit the Outdoor Retail industry tradeshow, The Consumer Electronic Show, and a few other marine and sporting goods shows.

A key to success in business is being in the right place at the right time. Nowhere is this more evident than at industry tradeshows. Every market or business has some type of industry only tradeshow where manufacturers exhibit their products and buyers for retail stores, catalogs, and distributors come to learn about them. As a rule tradeshows are expensive to attend as an exhibiting manufacturer, but they are extremely important. When creating your business plan it is imperative that you budget the funds necessary to exhibit at a few tradeshows. Almost all of the major retail or catalog accounts for the Cell Safe product were first met at a tradeshow.

Having a nice looking display and a professional appearance at a tradeshow will give you a tremendous amount of credibility with the buyers. If you make the commitment to go to a show, spend the time and money to create the right appearance. You will have all of the key industry people in attendance, it is important that you take advantage of this opportunity to promote your product and to build sales.

Before attending a show you should have a detailed plan of what you hope to accomplish while you are there. An important part of this plan is to do some homework before you go to the show. Figure out which buyers you want to talk to. We would call our target contacts before a show. Invite them to the booth, send samples, send postcards, you name it. Anything to get the product into their heads, before a face-to-face meeting. We wanted the meeting to be about the deal, not about presenting the product. We wanted them to understand the value before we ever met, or talked to them.

This section started off talking about Sales. We used a well-timed multi-prong approach to gaining sales. The Midnight Entrepreneur must become well versed in these three distinct areas:

- PR: Appearances in magazines gave us credibility and exposure
- Cold Calling: We called the major retailers in our target markets (Outdoor, Marine, Bike, Gadget)
- Trade Shows: Going to shows was key to getting face time with the big time buyers. We met hundreds of smaller retailers, which were often quick to order. The little guys kept us in business until we could close a bigger deal.

Midnight Advice on Quitting

In this chapter I make mention of realizing that I would soon need to quit the day job. At some point in the process, you too will come to this crucial juncture. My advice to everyone on this topic is to carefully plan this transition. Depending on your responsibilities and family life, this decision will have different consequences.

When I reached this decision point, I was single, lived alone, and had very few financial responsibilities. I had also saved as much money as possible in the prior months. My biggest concern was paying for health insurance. But, we had sales revenue, and things were growing in the right direction. I was confident that it was time to make the leap. You should carefully list out and understand your financial commitments and needs before you make the leap. The more commitments you have, the longer you may need to wait.

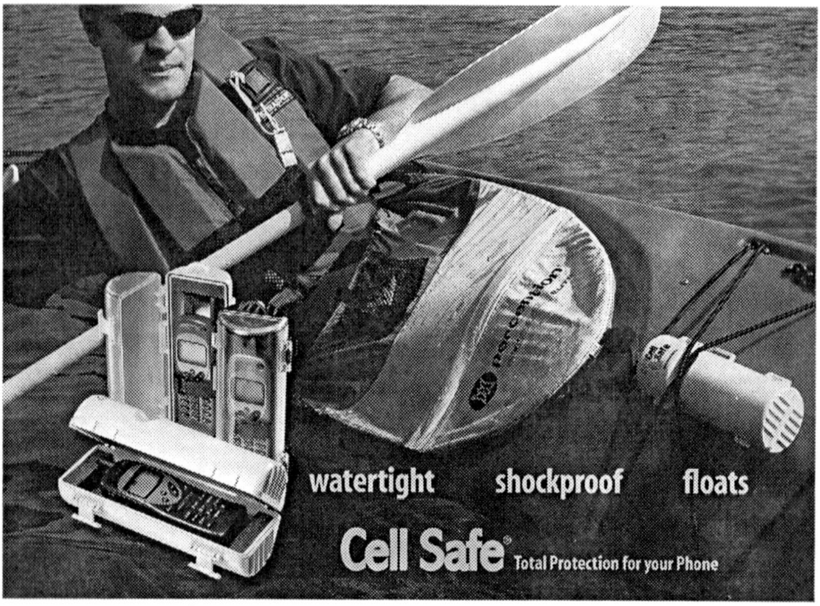

Cell Safe action shot postcard, used for direct mailings to retailers.

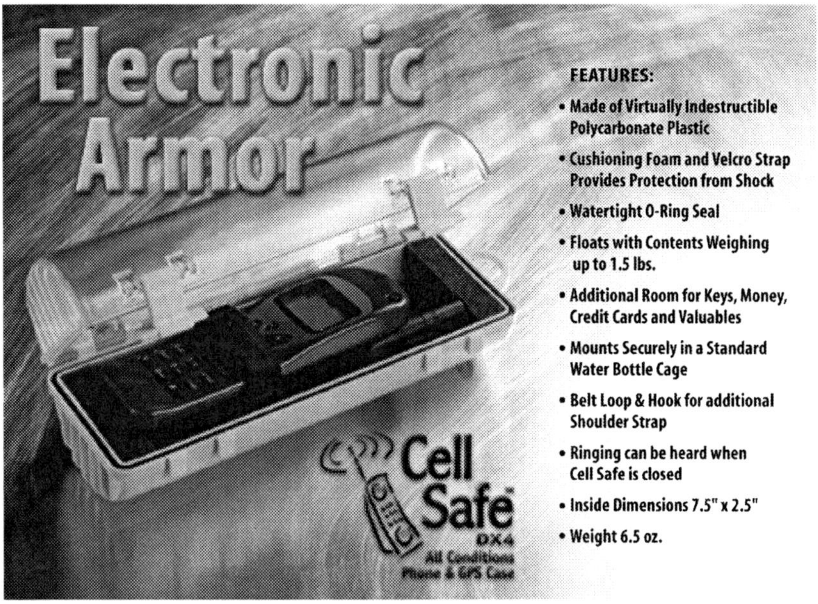

Cell Safe product data postcard, used for direct mailing and as a data sheet.

Chapter 8

Operations

Getting ready to fill your first order can be both an exciting and a chaotic time in the life of a start-up business. By now you have spent weeks, or even months, preparing for the process and getting everything lined up so you can start selling. The "operations" phase of a small business is important, and should not be ventured into lightly. Many businesses have failed because they failed to embrace an important philosophy: *strategic planning.*

IS STRATEGIC PLANNING NECESSARY?

"My business is very small. Do I really need to develop a plan like this?" The best response to this question is, "Only if you want to stay in business and prosper." Consider the following reasons for strategic planning.

- Technology and the fast pace of change are making business management more complex. Strategic planning will help you foresee and react quickly to market changes and help identify areas in which your business is lagging behind.
- Competition is becoming tougher. In most cases, small businesses find themselves competing with much larger companies — ones that know the benefits of strategic planning and practice it.

- From a defensive standpoint, it is important that you apply the same concepts to your operation.
- Good financial control alone is not enough to ensure your business's success. In addition to a budget, you need long-term goals to determine the future direction of your company.
- You can use strategic planning to involve employees in all areas of your business, so they share your goals.
- You can use your plan to communicate with bankers, who often do not understand the nature of your business. Bankers must be convinced that your company is in control of its future before they will lay their money on the line. A comprehensive plan aimed at sustained growth in sales and earnings can be very convincing.
- A plan is also very helpful in dealing with your suppliers, advertisers, attorney, accountant, auditor, investors and business consultants.

Your Idea Sounds Good, But Ask Yourself These Questions…

- What skills and experience do I bring to the business?
- What will be my legal structure?
- How will my company's business records be maintained?
- What insurance coverage will I need?

- What equipment or supplies will I need?
- How will I compensate myself?
- What are my resources?
- What financing will I need?
- Where will my business be located?
- What will I name my business?

The Cell Safe Story Continues...

The operation began rather humbly, in my one bedroom apartment. I had found companies to make the components, and print the logo on the product, but I had not yet outsourced anyone to do the assembly. In the fall of 98, we got our first placement, a mail order catalog in the bicycle industry.

Their first order came in early October, just around the first time the mold produced parts. I assembled the first 100 pieces over the course of a few late nights in my apartment. I packed them up and shipped them off. I went off to my day job very proud that morning. I came home that night to find another order for 100 more pieces on my fax machine. I was excited, but started to dread the assembly work. I struggled through this for a few weeks, but eventually I got some help putting them together. We had caught the Christmas rush for this catalog; it was great for sales, but really challenged my assembly skills.

I quickly got the assembly tooling fabricated and soon had the printing company also assembling the product. Part of my strategy was to have as little overhead as possible. I wanted to run everything from my apartment. Initially it ran very well. During the first year, the operation grew to include:

- Assembly Location. This company would assemble the product, and then store it for me. They would then ship it directly to my customers. This practice is referred to as 'Drop Shipping" We would send over the packing slip and shipping information and they would ship it out.
- Sales Office – The sales consultants operated out of the basement of one of their houses.
- My Office – Located in my apartment.
- Clerk Office – I hired a part time person to process orders, ship samples, and handle other logistical duties. This person worked from her home.

To make our operation work more smoothly, I utilized a number of Internet based tools. The Internet was a wild and crazy place in 1999. There were plenty of companies offering great tools for little or no money. I became an early adopter for a number of these tools. Many of these companies disappeared, but two types of tools became crucial for the virtual operation.

The first tool was Salesforce.com, an online contact manager solution. This is an online contact manager solution. This tool was used by the salesman to record the names and info on all of their clients and target accounts. The tool allowed one user to enter a note on an account, and assign another user a follow up task. The salesman would enter his conversation notes, and then enter a task for our other office to send a sample, or he would send the order information over to be entered into our accounting system. This extremely efficient solution allowed us all to use the same information, but be in four different locations.

The second tool that we utilized was Quickbase.com. Similar to Salesforce.com, this was an online tool, accessible anywhere you can get on the Internet. We created a database that shared the shipping information with the company that was storing and drop shipping the product. The company would receive our shipping instructions, and then upload the tracking numbers. This would allow a salesman who received an inquiry about an order to instantly look it up and determine its status. Quickbase was easily customizable and very affordable. Having this functionality helped us make sure all of the orders were delivered and provided us with a strong customer service tool.

Over time, we shifted production of the product to China. When this happened, the company that was drop shipping for us was no longer interested in doing the work. We then went to a more formal fulfillment company. We continued to use the Quickbase tool with this company. Eventually we broke down and rented our own warehouse, but not until we were in our fourth year of business.

Midnight Advice on Logistics:

- *If the product is small enough. Ship from your house.*
- *If it is not small enough to fit at home, use a fulfillment company. These companies will store and ship your product. They charge for their service, but it's almost always cheaper then renting a facility and doing it yourself.*
- *At some point, it may make sense to have your own warehouse. Wait until there is cash flow and then get a place that you can afford. It is better to be in a building that is too small, then to go under because you can't pay the rent. Don't sign a long-term lease, one-two year's maximum.*
- *If you get to the point where you need to hire a staff, start off hiring part time employees. I was very successful hiring stay at home moms, who were looking for part time "mothers hours" work. I learned that no one is more efficient than a mom.*

The operations plan had a few key points:

- Keep the operation virtual. No overhead; everything home based.

- Utilize the Internet to facilitate communications. Don't appear small; use the tools to pull off a big company impression
- Find the right people for the right positions. I'm not a salesmen, so I hired some. I'm no good at accounting details, so I hired a clerk. I can't do graphic design, so I hired a designer, etc....

Accounting

An important business topic that every first time entrepreneur needs to understand is basic accounting. If you are not familiar with accounting principles my advice is to buy a copy of Quickbooks, and sign up for a training session. Do this as early in the process as possible. Quickbooks is an easy to use accounting software package. Using it consistently will help you keep track of all of your expenses and product costs. It will track your revenue and sales. It will also help you efficiently process orders.

Check the cheat sheets at the end of the book for more information on accounting and order processing.

Chapter 9

Grow the Business!

By now you are no doubt chomping at the bit, and cannot wait to launch your own business. Hang in there; we are almost finished with the book, but these next sections are very important, so sit back, relax, and continue reading and learning!

Plan Before You Grow…

After deciding to start or expand your business, it's critical to take the necessary time to formulate a realistic path for yourself. In an increasing competitive world where businesses face an uphill battle, planning helps minimize the risks involved.

A Harvard University study showed that the amount of time spent in planning a business is directly related to its success. Owners spending six months or less ended up with an 80 percent failure rate. Those who took a year or more to plan ended up with an 80 percent success rate. Many new entrepreneurs don't realize the business plan is perhaps the most crucial document to develop during the planning stage because it tells a complete story about their business. A well-prepared and comprehensive business plan (updated every six months!) serves several purposes:

- It forces you to take an objective, critical and unemotional look at your business project the way an outsider would. It assists you in setting goals, and determining how workable and desirable your venture is.
- It is an important sales tool for raising capital from outside investors. These people are primarily interested in the future profitability and value of an enterprise. They need to be convinced that they will earn a substantial return on their investment within a few years.
- It is a starting point for a more detailed operational plan, and becomes an important management tool for monitoring the growth and performance of the firm and charting future directions.
- It is a virtual must when applying for a loan. To the lender, the plan reveals your evaluation of your venture's feasibility and reflects your management abilities.

Do Not Be Afraid To Ask For Help!

Turning to outside specialists to help avoid or solve problems is standard operating procedure for large companies. Yet with the exception of accountants and attorneys, many small business owners avoid using consultants, and thereby deny themselves valuable and timely advice. The problem many entrepreneurs face is how to afford professional help at the point when their need is greatest: usually when their financial resources are most limited.

But advice need not be expensive. In addition to professional consultants, sources of assistance include chambers of commerce, trade associations, specialty newsletters and magazines, and business libraries. Moreover, chambers of commerce and many financial institutions publish how-to books for a small fee or just for the asking.

How Well Do You Know Your Customers and Prospects?

The quickest and simplest way to grow your business is to get your current customers to buy more items from you. Having a plan and a system in place to analyze your current customers will be extremely beneficial. Ask yourself the following questions:

- Who are your current customers? (include age, gender, income level and geographic locale)
- What are their buying habits?
- How do your customers learn about your products/services? (newspaper advertising, direct mail, word of mouth, Yellow Pages)
- Why do your customers buy your products/services?
- What qualities do your customers value most? (selection, convenience, service, reliability, availability, affordability)
- What qualities do your customers like least? Can they be adjusted to serve your customers better?

- Who are your best customers?
- Are there prospective customers who need your product or service, but whom you aren't currently reaching?
- What is your market share? Is it expanding, shrinking or stable?
- Is your market growing, shrinking or stable? Is it changing in other ways?

More Important Questions

You should address some of these questions when you write your original business plan, but they become even more important once you are in business and are pushing for growth.

- What business are you in?
- What do you sell?
- What are your target markets?
- What are your marketing goals for next year? (include sales and profit goals)
- What obstacles might keep you from achieving these goals?
- What is your marketing budget?

The Cell Safe Story Continues…

This is an area where I think I mostly failed. I'll divide it into a few sections. Please read this information very carefully; I want you to learn from my mistakes. Many entrepreneurs are so caught up in the "I can't wait to get started" mode that they don't heed the advice of others who have made the journey before them.

LISTEN UP!
I HAVE MADE THE JOURNEY AHEAD OF YOU…
AND I HAVE MADE MISTAKES…
BUT YOU CAN LEARN FROM MY MISTAKES…
SO READ THIS SECTION VERY CAREFULLY!

New Products

One strategy for growing a business is to offer additional products that are similar to your first product. You should be able to leverage your experience and infrastructure to make different models of your core product to address different needs.

We launched the business with the original Cell Safe DX2 product. This was the all yellow case. For the first year this was our only product. For a variety of reasons, we decided to launch a clear version of the product. This was very successful. It gave the product a much better point of sale presence, and opened it up to GPS users. GPS is the abbreviation for Global Positioning System. A GPS unit is a handheld device, similar in size to a phone, that is used for navigation in the outdoors. This variation to our product line was a simple and cost effective addition. It utilized our existing tooling and did not require extensive investment.

Our next product offers a few lessons. We had numerous requests for a case similar to the Cell Safe, but for a Palm Pilot PDA. I did not want to invest in another mold, so I looked for similar products, that I could adapt to this market. I found a company with the right sized case, they agreed to private label it for me, and we launched it as the Electronic Armor PDA case. It wasn't a huge sales success volume wise, but it did offer profitable margins. I did not have to invest heavily in the product, and many of our existing sales channels picked it up. So lesson #1 is to ***not reinvent the wheel.*** If it's out there, see if you can modify it to fit your market.

Lesson 2 is a little different. Over time, the company that I was buying the product from realized that there was a huge market segment that they were not directly addressing. They modified the product, and started marketing heavily in this space. They went as far as lifting part of our product name. Also, over time their production cost went up too much for me to keep my pricing intact. So eventually I dropped the line. So, lesson #2 is ***if you don't own the product, you are at someone else's mercy.*** Be Careful.

After focusing on the waterproof case market for a while, I decided I wanted to make some products that would have a wider, mass market appeal. I developed two small accessory products. The ClipSafe and the KeyCover. They were both small ticket items that I was hoping to get into big box stores like Wal-Mart. The products were received well, but I never had the clout to get them into the big box stores. I later decided that my big mistake was straying too far from my core market of waterproof cases for tech products.

KeyCover, Reversible Keychain. Sleeve encases the keys and prevents them from rattling.

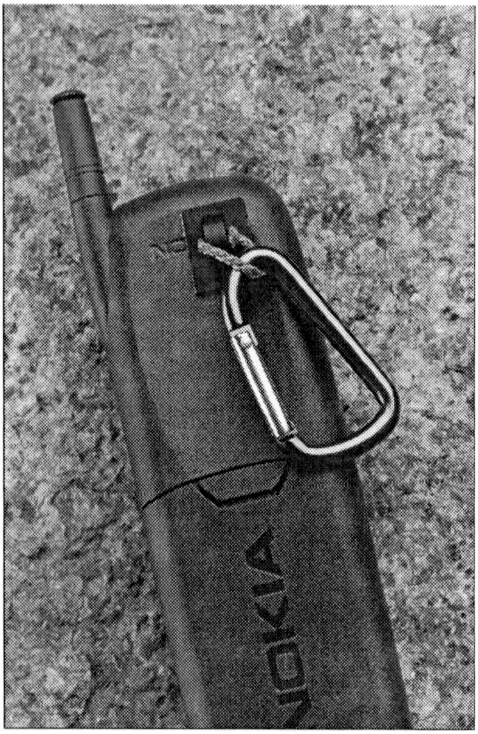

ClipSafe – Carabiner clip with mounting kit for attaching to the back of any phone.

With the lesson of not straying fresh in my head, I developed a new line of products called the Splashpac. This product line is a lower priced vinyl case that lets you use your device while in the case. The competitive edge for this product is its low price point and custom sizes for certain items that other companies don't make. This product line was just recently released, so there is no conclusion on its success.

SplashPac, Waterproof Phone Case

New Markets

In 2001 I tried to build sales for the Cell Safe products by getting into the advertising and promotional market. Our initial marketing plan called for using the Cell Safe for logo space. We had done a number of promotional orders for small companies over the first two years, and we wanted more of this business. So, we joined the ASI, (Advertising Specialty Institute), we went to their tradeshows, and advertised in their catalogs. We had a lot of interest from this segment, but not a lot of sales. We never made back our investment in this market. Our conclusion was that our product was not priced appropriately for this segment.

Also in 2001, we attempted to take our ClipSafe and Key-Cover into the mass market. We spent a lot of time and money trying to break into this market. We went to their tradeshows, but never closed the big deal. We never made back our investment in this market.

Cell Safe dressed up as a promotional tool.

Distributing Other Companies' Products

In late 2001 one of our distributors mentioned to us a new product being made over in Europe. This product was a waterproof hard-shell phone case that you can actually use the phone in. This had a huge competitive advantage over our Cell Safe. I did some research on the product, and determined that it would soon be coming to the US, and that I either had to be ready to compete with it, or I should try to work with it. So, I called the company and cut a deal to become their first US distributor. We started importing the product and did very well with it for the first year.

After the first year a bit of trouble developed with the manufacturer. Even though we had an agreement with this company, they signed an exclusive agreement with another company to become their sole US distributor. They encouraged me to work with this other company, but the pricing they offered pushed me out of the market. Just when I was threatening to sue the manufacturer, (an idle threat, since they being located in Finland would make it impractical), I came across another company in the US distributing the product. It turns out that the Manufacturer cut another "Exclusive" deal with another US company. This company was willing to sell me the product at a reasonable price, so I could continue to sell to my accounts. During this fracas, I stopped marketing the product, but I wanted to continue to serve accounts that we had already built. I continued buying product for another year or so. The two "Exclusive" distributors were both very upset with the manufacturer, but were stuck with a lot of inventory and are still selling the product. I eventually weaned my accounts over to the other distributor, and have since washed my hands of this line.

There are a few lessons here. The first is a good one. ***Sometimes its better to work with a competitor, than against them.*** This product was similar to mine, but it was at a higher price point. It served to compliment my product, and was accepted by many of my existing accounts.

The next lesson is a hard one, but similar to my PDA case. ***If you are selling someone else's product, you do not have total control.*** I spent a lot of time, money and effort promoting this product only to have the manufacture yank it away from me.

Your Second Product Will Define You !

Hopefully your first product idea will get you into business. But even before your first product hits the market, you need to start working on your second product. Very few single product companies succeed. Earlier in this chapter we talked about planning and understanding your customers. As you analyze your opportunities, be mindful that your next product will do a lot to define the direction of your company.

I had a few choices when I created my "Next" product. I choose to create the Electronic Armor PDA case. This product, like the Cell Safe, was a watertight, shockproof case. This product helped to define my company as a provider of waterproof cases for electronic devices. Had I chosen to create a non-waterproof phone case as a follow up product to Cell Safe, I would have been tagged as a cellular phone case company.

Understanding your niche is extremely important. It takes a long time to build a brand and a reputation within an industry. You need to get the most reward from your past efforts. Choosing new products that your current customers will accept is a great way to build sales. Our current Splashpac line of watertight protective cases reflects our effort to get back to the niche where we have had the most success.

Chapter 10

"Think like a Midnight Entrepreneur"

So far, I've shared the story of how, starting with negative funds, I took an idea and successfully built a business around it. Throughout the book I've shared bits and pieces of my Midnight Philosophy. By now you've heard enough to see a few themes. Keep expenses low, work hard, work smart, and don't quit the day job until you really have to. These themes are important, but another key to success is to learn how to think and to build your business in a way that allows you to react quickly to changing market conditions. One of the only natural advantages a small startup company has over the big guys is the ability to quickly and creatively address changes in the marketplace. The big companies have large bureaucracies that slow down the product development and marketing process. You must stay quick and focus on the niches that they overlook.

When you launch your product, at first it will be unique and you will get a lot of attention and hopefully sales will grow. But if you are successful, you will invite competition. You must be ready to compete. A tool that I've found helpful in both launching a product, and running a business is the concept of the OODA loop. Originally developed as a Military Strategy tool, the OODA loop is an effective concept for business and for life.

OODA stands for Observation, Orientation, Decision and Action. These four stages can be related to your development project as follows:

- **Observation:** Gather data about your market and your product concept, gather as much information as possible. Observe any item that you think is relevant.
- **Orientation:** Given your experience and understanding of the market, analyze the data. "Orient" your ideas and positions, develop conclusions.
- **Decision:** Based on your analysis, decide what you are going to do.
- **Action:** Put your plan to action. Execute.

After you execute, go back to Observation. Gather additional data about how your actions are affecting the market. Analyze the data and develop your next course of action.

The key to the OODA loop is move rapidly and to keep learning. Once you make a decision and then an action, there will be some sort of effect from your action. You must continuously observe your market and operation to ensure the effects of your actions are positive. You need to be learning and reacting at a quicker rate than your competition.

Recently I experienced a business setback because I failed at a critical point in the OODA loop.

After the success of the Cell Safe product, I developed SplashPac. This product is a low cost, soft sided, watertight case. There are a variety of sizes for specific applications, like phones, camera's, PDA's, etc.. The main competitive factor of this product is its low price point. I designed the product to meet the needs of the customer. Most people do not need a drybag that is submersible to 100 meters, they just need something to keep their electronics dry when a wave hits or the rain starts. We designed for this need, and have been able to market the product at very competitive price points. This product line has been profitable and fills a niche in the market. My failure comes with a planned item in the Splashpac line. No watertight cases for flip style cell phones existed in the market place. I went through the following cycles in my attempt to fill this void:

Round 1

Observation-I noticed that there were no watertight cases for flip phones on the market. I also knew that this was a very large market segment

Orientation – Based on my experience with other watertight cases, and my existing distribution channels, I determined that this was a good product for my company to pursue. I then came up with a concept for a watertight flip phone case that utilized the existing Splashpac technology.

Decision – I decided to proceed and create a prototype

Action- I created a functional prototype

Round 2

Observation – Initial prototype was tested, and tooling cost for production were obtained.

Orientation – Determined that some tweaks were necessary but that the design concept was sound.

Decision – This is where I stalled, I kept putting off the decision to make the production tooling and launch the product. I subsequently took **No Action.**

What makes the stalling point important is that a few months later a competitor came out with a watertight flip phone case that was nearly identical to my prototype. Had I made a decision and then acted quickly, I would have beaten them to market with the product. I believe the product concept was patentable. I have now abandoned this product. I do not want a conflict with their patent application.

The successful Midnight Entrepreneur must not get stalled in the cycle. It is okay to come to a decision point, and based on your assessment, decide not to pursue a particular idea or course of action. It is not okay to stall a decision or a waste time before acting. You must execute your plans. If you wait too long, someone else will beat you to the market.

Final Thoughts

Almost everybody understands that turning an idea into a successful business takes a lot of hard work, perseverance and a little bit of luck. The Midnight Entrepreneur increases his odds of succeeding by understanding the following ideas:

- Work smarter not harder. – By utilizing technology, leveraging other people's services, being clever, and being willing to learn; you will find ways to be more efficient and more effective.
- Keep the business lean. – By keeping expenses down your business will have the resources to invest in marketing and new product development. Keep the business virtual. Don't spend if you don't have to.
- Be willing to learn as you go. – You will never find a successful entrepreneur who will not admit that he has learned a lot along the way. Keep an open mind and absorb anything that might be useful.
- Be Patient, – I keep telling people that I'm getting rich overnight, but it might take me 10-20 years. Nothing happens quickly. You must have a vision, and you must not grow impatient or lose faith if things don't happen quickly.
- Don't let your Midnight endeavors interfere with your daytime performance. You must perform your job and perform it well. When it is time to leave, be honest with your employer. If you treat them sincerely, there

is a very good chance that they will be helpful and may even offer to take you back if your company fails.

- Maximize media exposure – The Midnight Entrepreneur must be a master of Public Relations. He cannot afford to pay for Media exposure, so he must find ways to get it free.
- Project a larger than reality image – You will be working out of your house, but your customers must never know this. Invest in decent marketing materials and have a strong message and corporate image. A good website is a must.
- Don't be afraid - You must have the confidence to execute. If you don't try, you will never succeed.

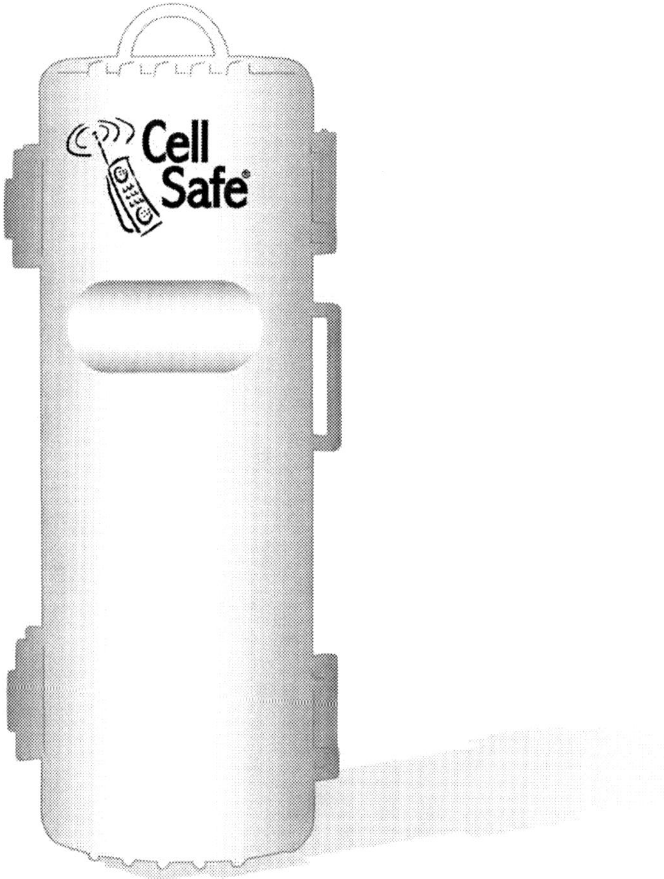
Cell
Safe®

Midnight Entrepreneur Cheat Sheets

"Other things you need to know"

Cheat Sheet # 1 *Website 101*

Every business must have a website. A good site will do the following:

- Explain quickly and clearly what the product is.
- Show how much the product costs.
- Explain how to buy the product.
- Explain who you are.
- Provide methods to contact you. Including a phone number. Make sure someone using the site can easily contact you. Hiding or not including an address or phone number will make you look small and shady.

Your website is an extension of your marketing materials. It should have the same look and feel as your brochures and datasheets. Most graphic designers are versed in website layout, you should try to have the designer that creates your marketing materials also create the website.

There are many ways to utilize your website as a sales and marketing tool.

- Enable your site to sell your product.
- Set up a dealer only area where your wholesale pricing is listed.
- Set up an image download area where catalogs, retailers and even magazines can download high-resolution images.

- Provide an area for consumer feedback.
- Provide a mechanism for consumers to join your mailing list
- Include product reviews on your site.

Cheat Sheet #2 *Marketing Collaterals*

You need good marketing materials. If you are a graphic designer you can create them yourself, otherwise hire an expert. These materials will be used to present the product to a potential retailer or end user.

Types of Collaterals

Product Images – You must have nice, high-resolution images of your product. Catalogs will request these images; they will also be useful for creating datasheets and catalogs.

Price Sheets - Contain basic product information, including MSRP and wholesale pricing. You may also have a separate price sheet that includes distributor pricing.

Order Form –Make it easy for a retailer to stock your product. Create a simple form that asks for all of their information and also lists all of your products along with wholesale pricing. Do not make the retailer look up pricing on another form. Include a fax number and your ordering terms.

Product Data Sheet – The data sheet will include as much information as possible about the product, including a nice product image. It should not contain pricing.

Postcards – This is a low cost version of the datasheet. Extremely useful for direct mailings. The postcard should have a product image on the front, and a brief description on the back.

Catalog – If you have a few products, you should make up a small catalog.

Logo – A nice logo will give you a professional look. Create a simple and to the point logo that works with your corporate image

Business Cards & Letterhead – Make up cards and letterhead that include your logo. These items are necessities if you want to establish credibility.

Cheat Sheet #3 *Pack List & Shipping Process*

When you ship that first order to a retailer, catalog or distributor, you need to follow a few industry standard processes. Hopefully by now you are using some sort of accounting package to keep track of your sales.

<u>Process For Customers that have Net Payment Terms</u>

1. In your accounting system, create a Pack List for the order. It must include the following:
   a. Customer name.
   b. Customer address.
   c. Product ordered.
   d. Quantity of product ordered.
   e. Shipping method
   f. Order date
2. Package up the product in a strong box. Using a self adhesive pouch, attach a copy of the pack list to the box. These pouches are readily available at office supply stores.
3. Ship the product using a service like UPS or Federal Express that provides tracking verification.
4. Once the product has shipped, you will mail to the customer an Invoice.

5. The invoice will include all of the information from the pack list, plus pricing information and information about their terms. It is also helpful to have a payment due date on the invoice.
6. Hopefully the customer will send you a check. When it arrives, note the payment in your accounting system.

If your customer pays up front, either by credit card, COD or check, create a receipt in your accounting system. It will look just like your invoice, except there will be no due date on it, and it will indicate that the order has already been paid. Ship this receipt along with the product.

Cheat Sheet #4 *Business Software*

You should have a software package for each of these areas:

Accounting - Accounting software is a must have item. You will use this package to track all of your expenses, inventory, sales, profit, etc… Get a package and learn it. I recommend the following:

- Quickbooks
- Netsuite

Contact Manager -You will use this package to keep track of your sales calls. Keeping good notes and using the software to remind you when to call again are just a few of the things this type of package can do.

Salesforce.com is my favorite contact manager solution.

Act or Goldmine are also good packages.

Shipping Solution – When it's time to ship product, make sure you do it the most cost effective and efficient way. Most shippers, including the Post Office, will provide free supplies and boxes. Use these tools to make shipping easy.

- UPS.com
- Fedex.com
- Stamps.com

Credit Card Processing – You must be able to take online and credit card payments. You will need a merchant account. Check with your bank first, they usually have the best deals. But you can also use Paypal to get started.

Productivity - Quickbase.com is one of my favorite tools. This site allows you to make custom online databases. This is a great way for keeping track of information within a virtual company.

Cheat Sheet #5 *Other Things You Need to Know*

True Cost Of Manufacturing

If you are making a product yourself, or if you are outsourcing it, you must understand your true cost of manufacturing. Don't forget to include the following items:

1. Inbound Shipping Costs
2. Taxes & Duties
3. Product Packaging
4. Shipping Packaging & Supplies

UPC Code

If you hope to sell your product at any major retail outlet, you will need to get a UPC code. This is the barcode that goes on the product packaging. The Uniform Code Council assigns these codes. It is not expensive, but you should get your code as soon as possible, and include it in your packaging design. For more information, visit:

www.uc-council.org

Liability Insurance

If you want to go to a tradeshow or get your product into the major retailers, you must have Liability Insurance. Contact a local insurance agent to get a quote. This is a mandatory cost of doing business. You should include funds for this insurance in your business plan.

Patent & Trademark Search

You can conduct online patent and trademark searches at the US Patent Office website.

www.uspto.gov

Cheat Sheet #6 *Online Resources*

Market Research

- Tradepub.com - Free trade journal subscription site

Product Development

- ThomasRegister.com – Listing of all types of manufacturing companies.
- USPTO.gov – Patent and Trademark Office site. Conduct online searches.
- Mfgquote.com – Source for getting manufacturers to bid on your project. Only for those with detailed CAD designs.

Marketing

- Tradeshowweek.com - Tradeshow directory
- Medialistsonline.com – Build a list of media outlets to send your press release.
- Modernpostcard.com – Postcard printing and direct mailing
- Megacolor.com – Brochure printing

Website

- www.godaddy.com - Domain name search and registration
- Yahoo Merchant Solutions – Best way to get an e-commerce site up quickly
- google.com/ads -Online advertising

Cheat Sheet #7 *Master checklist*

1. Pick an idea
2. Proof of concept
3. Research idea
4. Patent search
5. Prototype
6. Patent application (provisional)
7. Determine cost to manufacturer
8. Determine packaging method/design
9. Pictures of prototype
10. Market research
11. Select product name
12. Create marketing literature
13. Business plan
14. Decision point (go or no)
15. Set up business entity
    a. Incorporate
    b. Business phone & fax line
    c. Purchase domain name
    d. Business address
    e. Insurance

16. Secure funding
17. Choose a contact manager
18. Choose an accounting package
19. Create operations plan
20. Apply for Trademark
21. Set up website
22. Start PR effort
23. Start selling (calls, tradeshows)
24. Start production
25. Formal patent application
26. Start shipping product
27. Start cost reducing product
28. Start working on next product idea

Acknowledgements

Special thanks to:

Bonnie Bowes, Jim & Betty Bowes, Mary Ellen & Karen Bowes, Susan & Joe Harrington, Howie, Bunny, Glenn & the rest of the Fernald Family, Scott & Laura Taylor, Oscar Patino, Sam Sasso, Aimee Carbone, Advantage Plastic Products, Taitronics, Innovative Marking Systems, Tony G, Ed & Amy Kurja, Skip Winter, Professor Merrill Ebner. John Riddle, Karen McCormack, Ipswich Cooperative Bank, Peter Kim, Susan Bishop, Carla & Mike Abate, Michael and Julie Ellenbogen, Patrick Reavey, Doug Freeman, Neighbor Ray & Family, Chris & Aida Lashua, Joe Piccolo, Nancy Norton & the rest of the Family, Friends & Fools.

Printed in the United States
122543LV00001B/173/A

9 781598 580372